FINANCIAL MANAGEMENT SERIES | NUMBER 99

The Financial Executive's Job

With a Section on
Criteria of Good Financial Management

AMERICAN MANAGEMENT ASSOCIATION
330 WEST 42nd STREET, NEW YORK 36, N. Y.

Building a Competent Financial Organization

¶ **C. J. Kushell, Jr.**

Director of Finance, The Port of New York Authority

I HAVE OFTEN heard the thought expressed that many industrial management principles and techniques cannot be applied, or applied effectively, in public agencies. Let me explain briefly why they do apply in The Port of New York Authority. We are an agency of the States of New York and New Jersey. Established by treaty in 1921, the Authority was made responsible for developing public terminal and transportation facilities in the Port District and for promoting and protecting commerce moving through the metropolitan area of northern New Jersey and New York. The Port Authority is governed by a policy-making board of 12 Commissioners, six of whom are chosen by the Governor of New York and six by the Governor of New Jersey. Commissioners serve for terms of six years, and they receive no compensation or fees of any kind for their services.

The public terminal and transportation projects financed and operated by the Port Authority are, by their very nature, marginal projects or projects which require long periods of development. The Port Authority undertakes these necessary public projects only when private capital cannot finance them and only where the projects are capable, in the long run, of becoming self-supporting.

This requirement of self-support is based on the fact that the Port Authority has no power to levy taxes or assessments, and it may not pledge the credit of the two states. It sells bonds solely on its own credit and upon its ability to develop the revenue potential of the public facilities it constructs and operates.

The Port Authority's terminal and transportation facilities include the three well-known Hudson River vehicular crossings—the Holland and the Lincoln Tunnels and the George Washington Bridge; the three Staten Island Bridges; and the 16-story Port Authority Building which is a less-than-carload rail freight union terminal. Since 1944 the Port Authority has assumed responsibility for the operation, construction, and rehabilita-

¶ **THE AUTHOR**

C. J. Kushell, Jr., a graduate of Bucknell University, was appointed to the newly created post of Director of Finance of the Port of New York Authority on Dec. 1, 1951, after having served as Controller since 1947. He began his career as a member of the staff of Ernst and Ernst and then served as Auditor, Accounting Supervisor, and Assistant Personnel Director at Firestone Tire and Rubber Company. He was Personnel Director of Cudahy Packing Company; Assistant Controller, American Bridge Company; Procedure Supervisor, Carnegie Illinois Steel Company; and Controller and Assistant Treasurer of De Laval Steam and Turbine Corporation. He is President of the New York City Control and a National Director of the Controllers Institute of America.

CONTENTS

Copyright 1952 by the American Management Association, Inc.

These papers were presented at the Financial Management Conference of the American Manage-
Association held at the Waldorf-Astoria, New York City, November 29-30, 1951.

Papers are selected for inclusion in the *Financial Management Series* with a view to presenting
-ial of lasting reference value and general interest, and of meeting specific needs in the existing
of AMA literature. Where timeliness of subject matter makes immediate release to the member-
desirable, conference discussions may be printed in other AMA periodicals or publications. All
ssions, however, are summarized in *The Conference Reporter.* Information of unusual significance
ht out in the informal audience discussion periods following delivery of conference papers is later
rated in the published papers, or, where this is not feasible, may be appended to the paper in
ion-and-answer form.

The object of the publications of the American Management Association is to place before the
ers ideas which it is hoped may prove interesting and informative, but the Association does not
sponsor for views expressed by authors in articles issued in or as its publications.

● [*The price of this publication is*
$1.00 (members), $1.25 (non-members)] ●

ion of the Grain Terminal and Columbia Street pier at Gowanus Bay, Brooklyn, the world's two largest union truck terminals; the new Port Authority Bus Terminal in the Times Square area; the four metropolitan airports—New York International, La Guardia, Newark, and Teterboro; and Port Newark, a seaport with 22 deep-water cargo-working berths.

Starting in 1947, the activities of the Port Authority not only greatly increased but became widely diversified. During the last four years we have undertaken four new enterprises, i.e., airports, truck terminals, a bus terminal, and a large marine terminal. Thus, we have experienced the growing pains of expansion and have had to meet the tough problems inherent in managing widely divergent operations which are marginal financially. Our problem can be easily understood if you imagine your company embarking on the development of four new major products, all with different markets, trade practices, and manufacturing problems.

This brief explanation indicates that our management and financial problems are almost identical with those of industrial corporations, and we both solve these problems by using similar techniques. Like the successful industrial corporation, we have developed a strong, competent financial organization as a prime requirement to solve such problems.

THE MEDICINE MAN OF BUSINESS

Our concept of a strong, competent financial organization involves more than sound organization, an adequate number of competent employees, the proper assignment and description of duties, efficient procedures and written instructions, and modern accounting machines. These aspects of financial organization and management are important, but they are only a first requirement. Over and above these considerations, a strong, competent financial organization can exist only when top management delegates sufficient authority and responsibility to the chief financial officer and in turn makes full utilization of, and places sufficient reliance upon, the information, advice, and counsel of the financial organization in making management decisions and policies.

Think back for a moment to your reading as a boy. Do you remember the Medicine Man of the Indian tribe? The most promising youths were elected to undergo long, rigorous and intensive training for that job. All the records, traditions, the hard-learned wisdom of generations were in his keeping. He advised when the corn was to be planted and how much—when to migrate and where—when to make war and conclude peace. He read the omens, propitiated the evil spirits and invoked the good ones. A Tribal Chief was chosen for various reasons—heredity, powerful alliances, bravery in battle, or because he was the natural and acknowledged leader. But behind him as counsel stood the Medicine Man—continuing symbol of the past and interpreter of its bearing on the future. His name never went down in history, but his influence may have changed it. A competent financial organization should be the Medicine Man of business. It should function as a combination of historian, consultant, and prophet.

The management of The Port of New York Authority expects its financial organization—its Medicine Man—to carry out the concept of historian, management consultant, and prophet. Management wants our counsel and

advice on every major decision. They may not follow this advice—that is management's prerogative—but it is an integral part of the decision-making process.

The job descriptions of our Comptroller and Treasurer spell out this concept in clear language.

THE COMPTROLLER'S DEPARTMENT

The Comptroller's Department is under the direction of the Comptroller. The immediate staff of the Comptroller includes the Deputy Comptroller, who is authorized to act for and in behalf of the Comptroller and assumes responsibility for directing all activities of the Department in the absence of the Comptroller, and the following division heads: Chief Accountant, Budget Officer, Insurance and Claims Supervisor, Internal Audit Supervisor, and Procedure Supervisor. The Comptroller is authorized to take any reasonable action necessary to carry out the responsibilities assigned to him so long as it is consistent with his authority and with Port Authority policies and practices as set forth in the By-Laws and the Administrative Manual, and established by the Executive Director and the Director of Finance, and is consistent with sound business judgment.

Under the direction of the Director of Finance, the Comptroller has the following major responsibilities:

1. Develop, install, supervise, and maintain a comprehensive accounting system, conforming to generally accepted municipal and corporate theory and practice, reflecting the condition of the Authority's assets, liabilities, and financial transactions. Supervise the preparation of, and approve all official corporate books of account, official statements, and reports. Issue and maintain a Master Manual of Accounts and approved codifications.

2. Issue periodic financial reports on various phases of Port Authority operations, accompanied by appropriate written or verbal interpretations, charts, and recommendations; prepare and certify an Annual Financial Report covering Port Authority operations and financial position.

3. Acting for the Executive Director, verify financial data released to the public concerning Port Authority operations.

4. Advise the Director of Finance on all matters relating to Port Authority accounting policy, and on revenue, expenditure, trends, and developments related to Port Authority operations and their effect on the Port Authority's financial status.

5. Supervise the development and execution of an effective program of budgetary control. Direct the preparation of the annual budget covering all activities of the Port Authority for submission to the Board of Commissioners prior to the beginning of each fiscal year, and supervise the execution and control of the budget.

6. Develop and maintain an insurance program which will properly and adequately protect the property of the Port Authority against loss or damage arising out of insurable hazards.

7. Direct an effective and adequate system of internal control over the Authority's assets, liabilities, operating and capital transactions. Direct continuous internal audit of all accounting, financial, and related records of the Port Authority wherever located to ascertain that all revenues to which it is entitled are received; that all assets are properly accounted for and safeguarded from loss; and that established policies, principles, and procedures are adhered to.

8. Direct the maintenance of adequate property records to determine that all sums expended for purchase of property of any kind are within authorized appropriations and are properly accounted for; develop Port Authority depreciation policies and practices.

9. Establish and maintain an adequate cost-accounting system to produce the necessary records and reports for management use in analyzing and evaluating facility operations and in measuring the effectiveness of rate- and tariff-setting policies; accumulate appropriate cost data for utilization in connection with rate and tariff setting; conduct special studies as assigned.

10. Direct the preparation, issuance, and maintenance of a departmental manual of standard-practice instructions setting forth administrative policies and procedures relating to the Comptroller's Department; review forms to insure standardization and elimination of duplication; recommend administrative procedures for new facilities; when directed by the Office of the Executive Director, or upon request of any department, investigate Port Authority office and administrative procedures and operating practices, equipment, and systems; prepare detailed survey reports and recommendations for improvements.

11. Review proposed rates and tariffs, prior to their recommendation for adoption, as to inclusion of actual and estimated costs used, and recovery thereof, and as to administrative problems related to their enforcement.

12. Prepare, furnish, and interpret financial and statistical reports and records on various phases of Port Authority operations required in connection with economic analyses of new projects or facilities to insure that current information is available to all levels of management responsible for tariff setting and estimating.

13. Approve for payment and/or countersign all checks, promissory notes, and other negotiable instruments of the Port Authority signed by the Treasurer or other officers authorized by the By-Laws or designated by the Board of Commissioners. Examine all warrants for the withdrawal of securities from the vaults of the Port Authority, and determine that such withdrawals are made in conformity with the By-Laws and regulations established by the Board of Commissioners.

14. Ascertain that financial transactions covered by the minutes of the Board of Commissioners and the Committees of the Board are properly executed and recorded.

15. Cooperate with and assist independent accountants selected by the Board of Commissioners.

16. Delegate authority to division heads of the Comptroller's Department to enable the carrying out of their respective responsibilities and objectives, defining such authority and its limitations in writing.

17. Keep informed on the latest and most effective accounting and control techniques to determine that the most efficient methods are used by the Port Authority.

18. Conduct special studies or investigations as assigned by the Executive Director and the Director of Finance.

THE TREASURY DEPARTMENT

The Treasury Department is under the direction of the Treasurer, whose staff includes the Assistant Treasurer, the Cashier, and the Credit Manager. The Assistant Treasurer is authorized to act for, and in behalf of, the Treasurer and to assume responsibility for directing all activities of the department in his absence. Under the general direction of the Director of Finance, the Treasurer has the following major responsibilities:

Planning

1. Maintain a cash budget forecasting cash receipts and disbursements based on the current budget estimates and other available sources.
2. Prepare and maintain a long-range financing program, giving effect to all approved studies and assumptions of future construction.
3. Correlate borrowing requirements, both long-term and short-term, in the light of the construction budget, the long-range financial forecast of revenue and expense estimates, sinking-fund requirements, and existing debt structure.
4. Recommend financing programs relating to proposed new projects and facilities.

Financing

1. Advise the Director of Finance on timing and all other aspects of Port Authority financing, the status of the financial market, and other matters pertaining to the Port Authority's capital structure.
2. Recommend the type of security most desirable for the Port Authority's borrowing requirements, after giving due consideration to the conditions in the money market, existing debt structure, and sinking-fund requirements.
3. Cooperate with the Law Department in the preparation of official statements, agreements with underwriters, and other legal documents and matters pertaining to the issuance of Port Authority obligations.
4. Negotiate agreements and contracts with paying agents, registrars, and other fiscal agents.
5. Conduct negotiations with banks for short-term loans.

Relation with Banks and Investment Dealers

1. Conduct sales and promotion campaigns to assist investment bankers in the distribution of Port Authority bonds.
2. Maintain close contacts with banking and investment houses for the dissemination of financial information of the Port Authority, and promote among officials of such institutions good will for the Port Authority, as well as confidence in its management policies.

Investments

1. Formulate and recommend, from time to time, an over-all policy of investment of Port Authority funds, including sinking funds.
2. Recommend the purchase and sale of securities in the open market.

Custody of Assets

1. Maintain custody of all liquid assets of the Authority, including bank deposits and moneys temporarily in the possession of agents, collectors, and other employees.
2. Maintain full and accurate account of all moneys received and disbursed daily.
3. Maintain custody of all cash and securities pledged by tenants, contractors, and others as security under leases, permits, and contracts, and keep accurate records thereof, as well as a record of all performance and surety bonds deposited under the terms of such leases, permits, and contracts.
4. Recommend depositories for the establishment of bank accounts and negotiate the agreements therewith.
5. Recommend institutions to serve as custodians of securities owned by the Port Authority, and negotiate the terms of such custodian contracts.
6. Maintain a petty cash fund for cash advances and reimbursements.

Credit Management

1. Develop and administer the credit policies of the Port Authority.
2. Control the amount of credit extended by the Port Authority; gather and interpret credit information; follow up credit accounts and recommend action to be taken on delinquent accounts.

Signature and Endorsements

1. Endorse for collection and deposit to the credit of the Port Authority all checks, drafts, certificates of deposit, and other negotiable and non-negotiable commercial paper.
2. Sign all transfer warrants; countersign checks or drafts in excess of $10,000 and sign checks or drafts in the amount of $10,000 or less without cosignature. (Except payroll checks delegated for convenience to Comptroller's Department.)
3. Sign, together with any other officer or officers designated by the Board of Commissioners, all bonds, notes, or other obligations authorized and issued by the Port Authority.

Toll Tickets

1. Order, stock, and control distribution to facilities of all classifications of toll tickets and scrip.
2. Maintain a sales point for the sale of toll tickets and scrip and for the payment of authorized refunds.

Debt Administration

1. Maintain records showing the history of fiscal transactions and the amount of bonds, notes, and other obligations currently outstanding.
2. Request the Comptroller to prepare vouchers for the payment of principal and interest, when due, on outstanding obligations.
3. Maintain a record of payments of principal and interest and forward to the official files maintained by the Secretary all certificates of cremation of bonds and coupons paid. Maintain a current record of all past-due bonds and coupons which have not been presented to the paying agent for payment.

Reports

1. Prepare periodic reports on cash and investments, funded debt, and debt service for inclusion in General Data Book.

If, in the growth of a business organization, the number of day-by-day responsibilities and decisions required of the Comptroller and Treasurer become so great that insufficient time remains for the important function of long-range financial planning, then it becomes necessary to set up some method or mechanics by which this responsibility is given its proper emphasis. Our solution took the form of creating the job of Director of Finance.

THE DIRECTOR OF FINANCE

Under the direction of the Executive Director, the Director of Finance has the following major responsibilities:

1. Act as the chief financial officer of the Port Authority and supervise the activities of the Comptroller and Treasurer.
2. Administer and coordinate the financial affairs of the Port Authority.
3. Advise the Executive Director on all aspects of finance, including: (a) Policy matters relating to current and long-range Port Authority financial operation and

management. (b) Policy considerations concerning the source and disposition of Port Authority funds. (c) The economic and financial aspects of major studies, proposed acquisitions of new facilities, new construction and major leases and permits, including their effect on current and future revenues and financial position. (d) Policy matters relating to Port Authority accounting, budgeting, insurance, internal audit, procedures, and treasury functions. (e) Data contained in all financial reports of the Port Authority.

4. Report and interpret the effect of external economic and financial forces and influences as they affect the Port Authority operations.

5. Insure adherence of Port Authority financial and accounting policies to statutory requirements, and to actions of the Board of Commissioners and its committees.

6. Determine the adequacy of current financial reports and the need for additional reports.

7. Act as representative of the Executive Director in dealings with independent accountants selected by the Board of Commissioners.

8. Conduct special studies or investigations and assume additional duties as may be assigned by the Executive Director, and serve as a member or in an advisory capacity on committees to which designated.

You will note that this job description does not in any way de-emphasize the responsibilities of the Comptroller and of the Treasurer for the day-to-day operating decisions of the financial organization. The job is of an advisory nature—to review and measure with professional detachment the day-to-day operations, decisions, and trends in their relation to long-range goals, as well as to relieve the busy chief executive of as many financial management decisions as possible.

The temptation is great for the capable executive to try both to operate and plan. Few who try it achieve complete success in either function.

DELEGATION OF RESPONSIBILITY

By this time it should be abundantly clear that our financial organization does not actually control anything other than the administrative decisions within our own department. Under our concept it is still the Medicine Man.

This concept of financial organization imposes on our department a very heavy responsibility through all levels of supervision. The Port Authority believes in the principle of delegation of decision-making to the lowest possible level of supervision. We have worked hard on this principle and have achieved some degree of success. One of the most important aids in effecting delegation of responsibility and authority has been the development of responsibility accounting and budgeting.

Responsibility accounting means the collection, recording, and reporting of expenditures by the activities or functions of organization units. Organization units are the lowest level of management groups of persons to whom responsibility is delegated for carrying out activities under the control of that unit's supervisor. The accounting records we keep reflect such responsibility.

Every item of expenditure must be approved and accepted by an organization unit, and the Authority's system of budgetary control ties in directly with its accounting system and this principle of responsibility. Object classifications are not set forth separately. That is, separate accounts are not maintained for payroll, materials, rent, telephone, etc.

Rather, these items are included in the appropriate activity account f the organization unit concerned, and are available, naturally, upon nalysis. Each unit is given a job to do, is authorized a certain amount of noney with which to do it, and is controlled by the performance of that ob within the budgetary allowance, regardless of how the individual lollars are spent.

INCREASING SUPERVISORY EFFECTIVENESS

One of the major objectives in all our financial planning has been to ncrease executive and supervisory effectiveness and reduce the clerical ost of preparing essential control information by using the following nethods:

1. Reducing the volume of control information to a digestible amount through elimination of unnecessary reports and reports whose value is not commensurate with their cost.

2. Plugging any holes in the information structure by insuring that each level of management is receiving the reports it really needs to control the activities and results for which it is responsible.

3. Making certain that the whole system of control reports is integrated so that subsidiary reports (details) easily tie into major reports (summaries).

4. Improving the usefulness and timeliness of essential reports.

5. Setting up a permanent procedure for planning and controlling the Authority's system of reports on a continuing basis in the future.

THE NEED FOR CAPABLE PERSONNEL

Up to this point, I have discussed only the framework which we believe is most efficient. Yet, while the framework is essential it is not an end unto itself. All organizations operate through people, and the best framework is of little help without capable personnel with the will to make it work.

We must have competent, technically trained supervisory personnel. The "plus" in our case is the insistence on capacity for further growth in addition to the strong desire for that growth. This is the base on which we start to build. Given these factors, any failure is not the fault of the individual but rather that of his superior.

We believe so strongly in the necessity of a broad background for key personnel that we make every effort to develop it continuously. In fact, it is a Port Authority policy to encourage educational opportunities for all its personnel. In addition to the many training programs handled directly by our Personnel Department, any employee may add to his formal education at company expense if he satisfactorily completes the courses. Interpretation of whether the courses chosen relate to his job is on the liberal side.

QUALIFYING SUPERVISORS FOR MANAGEMENT RESPONSIBILITY

As in many companies, the majority of our expenditures for training have been for the nonsupervisory group of employees. Perhaps sufficient emphasis has not been placed on the training of supervisors.

In our department, all our supervisors actively participate in the

various technical organizations relating to their specialty. We go further and encourage training in nontechnical subjects which relate to their growth needs. How many times have you noted people in your own organization who are highly qualified technically but are lacking in the ability to translate their ideas clearly and concisely in laymen's language? All our supervisors have had formal training in report writing. At any time, they may be requested to conduct one of the weekly seminars organized on an interdepartmental basis. Although attendance at these sessions is voluntary, we have had to expand our original plans and organize sectional groups for nonsupervisory personnel. Where we feel a supervisor needs it, we encourage him to take a public speaking course.

This is very fine for the growth of the individual, but from the company's viewpoint the return on our investment comes only when the opportunity is provided for these increased capacities to be put to use. Our program is designed to supply these opportunities.

For example, we use our weekly staff meetings of the finance division heads not only for the usual reason of coordinating the activities of the financial departments, but as a training device. At each meeting there is a review of Authority-wide plans still in the formative stage. These men are encouraged to have an opinion and express it. In other words, they are getting some practice in the management decision-making processes. Careful minutes of these meetings are prepared, both to place the responsibility for action and to apprise the personnel below division level of action being taken or contemplated and to give them a sense of participation.

Another principle we practice is that of "Completed Staff Work"— defined as the study of a problem and the presentation of a solution in such finished form that all that remains to be done on the part of the next level of supervision is to indicate approval or disapproval of the completed action. The final test of this action should be "If I were the supervisor, would I be willing to sign the report I have prepared and stake my professional reputation on its being right?" This is a splendid double-edged training device. If a supervisor has to make too many changes in reports submitted for his signature, either he is failing in his training of the individual or that individual is not demonstrating capacity for further growth.

All levels of management receiving financial reports need guidance in interpreting the reported results. We financial men are prone to forget that financial reports can make dull reading to some executives, particularly if they do not understand them. Our job, therefore, certainly is not completed when the reports are issued. We must be satisfied that they come alive with meaning to the people for whom they are intended and that they are helpful to them in reaching their many management decisions. We do this by sitting down for a periodic review with each executive receiving these reports. While this helps the executives, another important aspect of such sessions is that it affords excellent training for our financial people in the management process.

There are many things that cannot be spelled out in a job description, but which add great value to the results of the financial organization and also better qualify the supervisor for further management responsibilities.

THE JOB OF THE INTERNAL AUDITOR

Our Internal Auditors, obviously, spend most of their time in the field, out of the department. The very nature of their assignments brings them in contact with all phases of the business. We consider that their job on any assignment goes far beyond the writing of a report indicating compliance or noncompliance with the rules of the game. That phase is basic, of course, but little of a constructive nature results if that is all that is done. We feel that a good job is done if the report outlines what was found wrong, what was done about it, and if it indicates that complete agreement has been reached as to the recommendations made. Remember that this is one of the important management tools and controls of any business. A department head should look forward to receiving the auditor's report because it is one of the few objective, impersonal reports that he receives on the performance of his own organization. There might be a situation in which everything is being done according to the rules of the game, but the auditor might find that those rules are outdated—that they are cumbersome or costly. His job is not completed until he has discussed this weakness with the Procedure Division and notified that division that something should be done to change the rules.

The same holds true in our Accounting Division. The basic codification of all expenditures is done in all departments throughout the company. To assume that everyone charged with this responsibility thoroughly understands the accounting system, may produce some misleading results. To make sure that the financial reports reflect the true conditions, it is necessary that representatives of this division be constantly in touch with the field forces, making certain that the people performing the original codification not only are performing their work accurately but, even more important, understand what the management is trying to achieve in its financial reporting.

THE IMPORTANCE OF SPECIAL REPORTS

To be of the optimum value the monthly financial reports must be issued as close to the end of the reporting period as possible. This imposes a time schedule that excludes any other considerations. Yet, probably the reports that are of the most value to management are not the fixed financial reports, but the special reports that pinpoint a specific problem area where the whole problem can be put in proper perspective.

We are constantly criticizing our periodic reports, attempting to reduce them to the simplest elements, but at the same time concentrating more and more on special reports, as we find management more receptive and better able to reach solutions to problems with this kind of approach.

CONCLUSIONS

The principles and policies I have been discussing have worked in the Port Authority. For example, when our Treasurer retired at the end of last year and, in addition, the job of Director of Finance was created, a wholesale chain reaction followed. The Deputy Comptroller moved up to Comptroller, the Assistant Treasurer to Treasurer, the Budget

Officer to Assistant Treasurer, the Internal Audit Supervisor to Budget Officer, and the Assistant Procedure Supervisor to Internal Audit Supervisor.

We would not have made these moves if we did not think that each man concerned was not only technically qualified to carry out the duties of the respective positions, but, through the training he had received, was ready for increased responsibility. We believe that the fresh viewpoint each of these men brought to his new duties will pay immense dividends. Each man took with him the knowledge of his prior position, which he can now pass along to his technically qualified assistants. Thus, each of these men automatically will become better qualified for further responsibility.

There is a lesson in history for practicing controllers and treasurers in what has happened to the Medicine Man. In some cases he is still the honored and respected historian, consultant, and prophet. In others, he has become merely a figurehead, dozing in the sun. Those are the ones whose predecessors—faced with problems, pressures, and influences outside their province—became jealous of their prestige and attempted to usurp the Chief's prerogatives. Dissension and subsequent lack of confidence in his motives and methods followed.

At the Annual Meeting of the Controllers Institute of America on October 1, 1951, E. J. Hanley, President of Allegheny-Ludlum Steel Corporation, voiced this warning: "Management is best served if the Controller continually bears in mind the service-department idea and avoids the temptation to make administrative decisions for departments outside his own division."

A financial organization has a specialized function in business. Let us concentrate and build well within that function.

The Place and Status of the Financial Executive Today

T. F. Bradshaw
Associate Professor, Harvard Graduate School of Business Administration

EVEN A QUICK glance at the status of the financial executive in management today reveals two things:

First, his status varies from company to company. In some companies he performs vital management functions and is considered part of top management. In other companies he is the chief accountant or head bookkeeper and, as such, has no claim to participation in top management. In these cases he is regarded as a necessary evil.

Second, his status is rapidly changing. In those companies in which he is a part of management, he is increasing his contribution to the management process. In those companies in which he is a bookkeeper, he is becoming more and more enmeshed in detail as the avalanches of paper work brought about by increasing government controls descend upon him.

Both these facts--variations in status and rapidly changing status—are well known to most financial executives. A good deal of talking, at least, is done about it.

Perhaps a sociologist would look at these observations and say, "This is a period of revolution." In many ways he would be right. Business management is undergoing a change, deep-rooted and far-reaching enough to deserve the term revolution.

What is the nature of this management revolution and how will the financial executive fare? These are the questions I should like to discuss.

It is easy enough after a revolution has occurred to write learnedly of exactly what happened—whose status was changed and why. Without the benefit of perspective, however, all we can do is observe bits and pieces and hope we are looking at the main stream rather than at side currents.

¶ **THE AUTHOR**

Dr. T. F. Bradshaw graduated from Harvard College in 1940, *magna cum laude*, and from Harvard Business School in 1942 with high distinction. After naval service in the Pacific during World War II, he began his teaching career at Harvard Business School and received his doctorate there in 1950. In addition to his position as Associate Professor at the Business School, he is Research Director of the Controllership Foundation. At present he is serving as special consultant to the Secretary of the Army.

THE NEED FOR A NEW WAY OF MANAGING

New ways of managing do not arise because a management theorist writes a book. They arise because the facts-of-life of business change, and, in order to survive, management changes with them.

What are some of these changes in the facts of business life which have occurred recently? I should like briefly to discuss two:

1. Profits are no longer the guidepost for most business decisions.
2. In most medium and large companies, the job of president has become too big for one man.

Neither of these statements is new or shocking. Many conferences and publications have paid considerable attention to spelling out the implications of these two basic changes in American management.

PROFITS AS A GUIDE

After teaching control and finance for several years at the Harvard Business School, I was recently given the assignment of developing and teaching a course in small business, or new enterprise. I found myself in a new world, and it was some time before I realized why. It was a world in which almost every decision was made in the light of profit and was quickly appraised by an inexorable test of profit. Why is this so different from my observations in large business?

Does this mean that large businesses are not involved in the pursuit of profits? Despite our recent preoccupation with other objectives, by far the most important social obligation of business is to make a profit. Only when management makes a profit can it turn its hand to so-called social benefits. When management does not make a profit, a large social disservice is done. This is the hard core of our way of life.

The making of a profit, then, is still the objective of each business, large or small. Who in the large corporation is motivated in his decisions by profit of the company? This is perhaps the crucial question. It does not matter if each member of management has sworn allegiance to the profit motive; are his day-to-day decisions motivated, sparked, tested, and appraised by the yardstick of maximum long-run profits for the company? In many cases the answer to this question must be no.

Let us look at some of the standards by which some executives make decisions.

THE SALES MANAGER

The sales manager's objective may be ever-increasing volume of sales. Perhaps he has a pet line of products; they must be pushed at all costs. Perhaps he envies his friends who are sales managers of companies with national distribution; his objective, then, is to blanket the country with his products. Perhaps he feels he does not have a large enough sales force; his objective may be to by-pass independent distributors and enlarge his own selling force.

Attaining these objectives may or may not result in profits for the company.

THE PRODUCTION MANAGER

Trained in engineering, the production manager may have a love for fine tolerances and may machine each part to the full capability of the tool. He may believe that a 5 per cent scrap loss reflects more credit on him as a manager than does a 15 per cent scrap loss. He may aim at a clean, over-maintained plant. To avoid production delays, he may aim at overstocked material bins or stand-by machines.

Attaining these objectives may or may not result in profits for the company.

THE ACCOUNTANT

The accountant's standard may be the number of errors which are found in his reports. Perhaps he is motivated by a desire to close on the seventh day of the month following, rather than the ninth. Perhaps he aims at mechanizing all accounting. If he is responsible for credit, perhaps his objective is the lowest possible credit loss.

Attaining these objectives may or may not result in profits for the company.

It seems clear that while the company itself is judged by profits, individual decisions may or may not add to profits. Each member of the management group is motivated by the surroundings of the world he lives in—the selling, production, or accounting world. These worlds supply their own standards. Decisions taken in accordance with these varied standards in many instances not only do not add to profits, but effectively insure that a profit will not be made. Management left on its own is unbalanced management.

Who then in a company lives in the world of profit? The president of the company, by virtue of his lack of attachment to a specific function, is at least in a position to live in the world of profit.

THE JOB OF PRESIDENT HAS GROWN TOO BIG

This brings me to the second force of circumstance which has created this management revolution. The job of president has grown too big for one man. Essentially his job is to bring balance to normally unbalanced management and gear the parts together so as to produce a company profit. This task has become far more than reconciling differences of opinion among members of the management group.

In simplest terms, the job of president is to set a profit goal for the company, interpret that goal in terms of standards of performance for each department, periodically take a sounding to see how each department is progressing, and constantly make adjustments throughout the whole structure.

Even when expressed in these oversimplified terms, it seems obvious that this is a task far beyond any one man. Or, more accurately, it can be performed by one man only when he receives considerable help in that basic task.

The earmarks of a revolution are with us. I have presented two factors that I believe have pressured management into new ways of doing things. The profit motive is no longer the spark plug for many business decisions.

Members of management, left to their own devices, make decisions on the basis of motivations and standards not necessarily related to profits. The logical source of balance and profit direction is the president. Because of the many and complex parts of the modern corporation, each spinning in its own orbit, this job is far too big for one man.

A NEW WAY OF MANAGING

What is this new way of managing which constitutes the core of the management revolution of our time?

First, it consists of organizing so as to push the profit motive as far down the organization as possible.

Second, it consists of adopting the concept of management planning and control.

Third, it consists of building an organization which can help the president carry out his job of coordinating the parts, and which can supply him with the tools of management planning and control.

DECENTRALIZING FOR PROFITS

Organizing to push the profit motive down the organization is dramatically illustrated by the recent reorganization of the Ford Motor Company. Up to 1946, the Ford Motor Company had been operated under the direction of a highly centralized management.

A spokesman for Ford management pointed out that under such centralized management, "A single net-profit figure combined the end result of all the strengths and weaknesses of the numerous individuals who guide the destinies of the company, but it provided no means by which the respective contributions of those individuals could be segregated and evaluated . . . In short, the organizational arrangements and the financial-control system were such that only a few top executives could be held responsible for the profit performance."

Ford management considered that decentralization was the obvious answer to the problem. At present there are six principal divisions of the company. Each division is treated as a separate company with full responsibility for costs incurred and sales volume achieved—in short, profit performance.

This, of course, is not an isolated example. The process of pushing the profit motive down as far as possible has been going on for some time in a number of companies.

MANAGEMENT PLANNING AND CONTROL

Responsibility for profit, however, can be pushed only so far down. In the Ford Company, an individual assembly plant has little or no control over sales volume, engineering expense, costs of purchased materials, and many other important elements of profit. Once profit responsibility has been pushed down as far as it can go, what is to insure that profit-making decisions are made below that point?

It is here, perhaps, that the evidence of the management revolution is most striking. It is here that those companies which share in the new way of management differ most markedly from those which do not.

The new way of management has been summed up in the phrase "management planning and control." By management planning and control, I mean acceptance of the importance and validity of certain objectives. These are the objectives: First, setting a profit goal; second, setting departmental goals which, taken together, will achieve the profit goal; third, measuring progress against those standards; fourth, making continuous adjustments to keep the whole organization moving in balance toward the goal. The tools of control are not nearly so important as a clear realization of the ends to be attained. Each company which has substituted navigational flying for seat-of-the-pants flying has developed its own kit of tools.

As far back as 1926, Albert Bradley of General Motors put his finger on what is, perhaps, the central tool, when he said:

> The financial control policies of General Motors Corporation serve two general purposes: (1) The pricing of the product in a manner consistent with the fundamental policies of the corporation as to return on investment; and (2) the maintenance of effective operating control through manufacturing schedules which are at all times in logical relationship to consumer demand. This requires not only the best possible estimate of future volume of business but also the maintenance of a healthy position in regard to: (a) inventory carried by the corporation and its dealers; and (b) purchase commitments for materials made by the corporation with its suppliers. The tool by means of which these policies are made effective is a comprehensive scheme of forecasting, combined with a systematic comparison of actual results with the forecast.

What Albert Bradley described in 1926 would today be called a profit budget. A profit budget is merely a systematic way of establishing an over-all profit goal; developing a plan of operations for all levels of management which gears in with the over-all goal; and providing a method whereby actual results can be compared with the plan in such a way that effective action can be taken.

The profit budget, however, is merely a framework. Within that framework, progressive managements make effective use of many other tools of control such as market research, production planning, statistical quality control, inventory control, and management-development planning.

MANAGEMENT PLANNING AND CONTROL IN ACTION

A profit budget, even when supplemented by a number of other control tools, does not adequately describe what this revolution has meant to some managements. The key lies in fitting the pieces together and observing management planning and control in action. This can best be described by an example.

In a large steel company, comparison of actual to budgeted profit revealed that a certain major product was falling behind its profit goal. The controller and the operating vice president outlined the plan of attack on the problem. The Sales Department reviewed volume of sales, participation in the market, comparative prices, discounts, advertising and selling costs. The Production Department investigated volume versus plant capacity, effectiveness of process and equipment, manufacturing difficulties, and scrap losses. The Engineering Department reviewed the design of the product and calculated the effect of the possible obsolescence of facilities and inventories if the design were changed.

Some of these analyses were based on information provided by operating budgets; others on market-analysis information; others on production- and facilities-planning information; still others were based on data freshly developed to meet the needs of the problem.

Throughout this entire management process, a cost analyst, a representative of the controller, stood by the shoulder of each operating man involved. Together with the operating man, the cost analyst studied the problem, clothing with figures the operating man's experience with people and things. He abstracted the facts from each department's experience, showing the interrelationship among departments.

All the material pertinent to this problem was then summarized by the Controller's Department and reduced to the alternatives of action which had been evolved from the studies of the operating departments. Each alternative was then presented in terms of its forecast effect on profits.

Top management reviewed the problem and the possible solutions and decided on a course of action. Responsibilities were assigned to each major executive. The controller's assignment was to devise and operate a system of follow-through to compare actual with estimated results of the approved plan.

This is management planning and control in action. It is teamwork effort to achieve a planned result.

PROVIDING THE TOOLS FOR PLANNING AND CONTROL

A third element of this management revolution is the building of an organization which can provide the president with the tools of planning, control, and coordination.

It is at this point that we return to the question suggested by the title of this paper—what is the status of the financial executive? A basic feature of all revolutions is that they change the status of groups and individuals. This management revolution will prove to be no exception. The key to the future status of the financial executive may perhaps be obtained by looking at the methods by which companies have organized to provide the chief executive with the tools of planning and control.

Companies have organized for this purpose in one or a combination of three ways:

1. Creation of a figure-analysis staff to report directly to the president.
2. Separation of figure-gathering, or accounting, from figure-analysis within the financial executive's organization.
3. Setting up figure-analysis staffs to report to the various functional vice presidents.

CONTROL STAFF FORM OF ORGANIZATION

Koppers' management considers it essential to the success of the com- ervell, is a well-known proponent of the "Control Section" form of organization. The Control Section is a staff group reporting directly to the president and is designed to provide the chief executive with more hands, more eyes and ears, and more hours per day. This concept has been ably presented in the past, and I shall treat it briefly for that reason.

Koppers' management considers it essential to the success of the company that definite objectives be set forth as goals and that definite plans be developed which will allow attainment of those goals. This is clearly a job of top management, yet one which requires detailed work beyond the capacity of an individual. The Control Section coordinates the development of plans by drawing together the forecasts and plans of each operating unit and staff agency. In cooperation with the finance group, it analyzes these plans in terms of the need for and availability of working capital and develops plans to obtain necessary funds. The Control Section tries to strike a balance between the necessity for expanded production and the funds which can be provided.

Departmental forecasts and operating plans are reviewed carefully by the Control Section in the light of historical results, independent forecasts of the general trend of business, and other factors. These programs are prepared to cover the coming calendar year, by months, in considerable detail. A program is concurrently developed covering ten years, by year, for long-range planning purposes. When finally consolidated and reviewed, these programs are recommended to the various management committees and to the chief executive.

In addition, the Control Section constantly reviews the organization of the company; analyzes work methods which affect more than one department; constructs progress reports which not only relate what has occurred but explain why it has occurred.

This is, perhaps, sufficient to indicate the functions performed by the Control Section and, by indirection, the kind of work done by the Finance Department. Though I have used only the Koppers Company as an illustration, this form of organization is appearing in more and more companies.

SEPARATION OF FIGURE-GATHERING FROM FIGURE-ANALYSIS

Separation of figure-gathering, or accounting, from figure-analysis within the controller's organization is well illustrated by the organization of the United States Steel Company. Throughout the United States Steel Company the controllers are responsible for both figure-gathering and figure-analysis. Each controller, however, is assisted by an analytical staff group called the Cost and Statistical Division.

This Division is charged with a threefold responsibility:

1. To point out to management where problems exist by investigation of accumulated historical facts.
2. To advise management on the effectiveness of the execution of their plans by analysis of factual records.
3. To aid management in decisions by assisting in the evaluation of alternative courses of action based on the best available facts.

For example, in the sales field the problems handled by the Cost and Statistical Division include profitability of products, pricing, competitive positions in various markets, the desirability of producing new products, and selling expenses.

The Cost and Statistics Division collaborates with the Engineering Department in planning expenditures for machinery, plants, mine, and other facilities. The alternate solutions for each project are evaluated by the Division. Factors considered include investment, relationship to market, methods of manufacture, raw materials sources, and assembly cost. After such expenditures are made, actual financial results are analyzed to check whether the anticipated results were actually attained.

The work of the Cost and Statistics Division of the Controller's Department in U. S. Steel, then, is not far different from that of the Control Section in the Koppers Company. Both are aimed at providing the president with the tools of coordination and department heads with the over-all company background against which to make decisions.

ANALYTICAL STAFFS FOR FUNCTIONAL VICE PRESIDENTS

I shall mention the remaining organizational development very briefly. In a number of companies the functional executives are building their own analytical staff groups. The sales manager is strengthening the Market Research Division. The production manager is broadening the Production Control Unit to include long-range facility planning, inventory planning, and possibly, planning for stabilized employment. The director of industrial relations is setting up a statistical unit to provide information for collective bargaining, pensions, health and accident insurance, and other benefit programs.

THE FINANCIAL EXECUTIVE AND THE MANAGEMENT REVOLUTION

In summary, then, the way in which management goes about its task is changing. I have called this change a management revolution because of its vast nature and the rapidity with which it is being accomplished. Its roots lie deep in two basic changes in business facts of life: first, that profits no longer constitute a sufficient standard of action throughout the modern corporation; second, that the job of president has grown too large for any one man.

The outward evidence of this revolution is threefold: first, companies have decentralized to push the profit motive as far down the organization as possible; second, companies have adopted a concept of management planning and control in order to throw the beam of profits throughout the organization; third, companies have organized special staff groups to assist the president in carrying out his job of gearing the parts together.

To accomplish this latter purpose, some companies have set up a staff group reporting directly to the president; others have separated figure-gathering from figure-analysis within the financial executive's organization; others have built staff groups reporting to various functional vice presidents.

What are the implications of this management revolution for financial executives?

There are undoubtedly organizational lessons to be drawn from the way companies have organized to meet the needs I have outlined. At best, however, a company's organization is a continuing compromise between principles and men. I am sure that General Somervell has had more influence on Koppers organization and Enders Voorhees has had more influence on U. S. Steel's organization than any set of organizational principles. The lesson does not lie in principles of organization.

What then is the lesson for the financial executive? Merely this—if the financial executive does not build himself to meet the needs of management, management will build around him. There is ample evidence that some financial executives have filled managements' need and have thereby emerged as members of the management team. There is also ample evidence that some financial executives have not.

There is a tide in the affairs of the financial executive. What must he do to take it at the turn?

First, recognize this management revolution in all its implications.

Second, realize that the developments of financial management over the past two decades have prepared him, better than any other officer, to provide the president with the planning and control tools he needs.

Third, broaden himself to increase his knowledge of the objectives of the whole company and the interrelationships of the parts.

Fourth, reorganize his department to free himself from the detail of routine accounting, tax work, and government reporting.

Finally, staff his organization with young men of broad management potential who can grow to meet the ever-increasing demands of management for a figure partner.

○   ○   ○   ○   ○   ○

The place and status of the financial executive will be determined by each financial executive in each company and within the next few years.

Criteria of Good Financial Management Under Current Conditions

A PANEL SESSION

Panel Chairman:

JULES I. BOGEN, *Professor of Finance, New York University Graduate School of Business Administration, and Contributing Editor, Journal of Commerce*

Panel Members:

ROBERT F. BRYAN, *Partner, J. H. Whitney & Co., New York*

HAROLD B. DORSEY, *President, Argus Research Corporation, New York*

ALVIN R. JENNINGS, *Partner, Lybrand, Ross Bros. & Montgomery, New York*

ROGER F. MURRAY, *Vice President, Bankers Trust Co., New York*

INTRODUCTION

By Dr. Jules I. Bogen (Chairman)

THE SUBJECT of this panel discussion is particularly important in the dynamic period in which we live. We all feel the urgent need for "Criteria of Good Financial Management Under Current Conditions." I should like to emphasize the second part of the title—"Financial Management Under Current Conditions."

What are current conditions? We live in a highly dynamic world in which the conditions of a year or two ago are no longer the conditions of today. In the newspapers, for example, we have read that one great industrial enterprise is arranging to borrow $300 million for a period of 30 years, and still another industrial enterprise is arranging to borrow $300 million for a somewhat longer period—100 years. If it were a railroad—if it were a public utility—we would not be surprised too much. But for a great industrial enterprise in the electrical industry, and for another in the chemical industry, to borrow $300 million for such long

THE AUTHOR

Dr. Jules I. Bogen has combined journalism with an academic career. He is Professor of Finance at the New York University Graduate School of Business Administration and has been Financial Editor, Managing Editor, and Editor of the *Journal of Commerce*. He is now Contributing Editor. He has served as technical advisor to the Senate Committee on Banking and Currency and is the author of numerous books and articles on banking, business finance, and taxation. Active in the affairs of the American Management Association for some time, he served for two years as Vice President in charge of the Finance Division.

[23]

periods means that conditions have changed. It would have been unthink-able ten years ago; it would hardly have been thinkable even a year ago. Yet incurring debt on so large a scale and for such long periods is just part of the grist of the day's news, today.

What are the new conditions that have brought about this great change in financing practice?

First, there are very high taxes. Taxes have been high for a long time. But taxes can be raised so high, we now can see, that the attractions of bond financing, as against other kinds of financing, can be too much for even the most virtuous of managements to resist—those managements that have hitherto paid little heed to the tax benefits of bond financing because they felt it was not a conservative or wise method for raising long-term capital.

There is also inflation, and the belief that rising prices will prevail for a long time.

Another new condition is the mounting faith in future economic growth. We added more people to this country in the last year than live in the city of Philadelphia; and, if the population experts are correct, in the next year we may add almost as many people as live in the city of Chicago. An expanding economy requires different attitudes and plans from those fitted to a stable economy.

Another related factor is the decline of the liquidity ratio in corporations. In the year ended June 30, current liabilities of all corporations rose by $19 billion, but their holdings of cash and government securities increased by only $2.9 billion. The liquidity ratio is clearly coming down.

Lastly, we are in a period of declining profit margins, reflecting rising costs and stable selling prices. Corporate profits in the aggregate in the second quarter of this year were fully one-third lower than in the final quarter of 1950. A one-third drop in profits in six months would have been considered catastrophic if it were not for the fact that they were so high in the final quarter of last year. Even as it is, the decline is highly significant.

Those are some of the new conditions affecting financial management to which our experts are going to turn their attention in this panel session.

I. INTERESTS OF THE INVESTOR AND MANAGER

By Robert F. Bryan

THE MEMBERS of the panel thought that it would be appropriate to open this discussion with a brief review of the main questions a risk capital investor would raise regarding a manufacturing company in which he was considering the purchase of a substantial stock interest. For the most part these are questions that financial officers are frequently called upon to answer regarding their own companies.

ANALYSIS OF SALES, COSTS, AND PROFITS

Selection of a company for further analysis is ordinarily made on the basis of a generally favorable outlook for the industry, the past record of the company, and evidences of potential future growth. The study of financial condition begins with a careful analysis of probable sales volume,

costs, and profits under different sets of assumptions regarding future conditions. Special points covered are the proportion of the sales dollar represented by value added in the company's own operations, as distinguished from cost of purchased materials; the relative proportion of costs that are fixed and variable; the direct labor-cost ratio; the variation of costs and profits with volume; the apparent break-even point; the strength of the product price structure; and the importance of selling as compared with manufacturing costs. The prospective investor also will want to know how wage rates paid by the company compare with those paid by other companies in the same industry and in the same general locality, and how soon it may be necessary to increase wages. Also, what important contracts for property, materials, or special services used by the company may have to be renewed at an early date and at what increases in prices? If there is short- or long-term debt, will it mature soon, and if so will it be necessary to refund it at higher interest rates?

After several years of wide price changes such as we have been experiencing, it will be important to know to what extent recent earnings reflect substantial inventory profits or losses. If inventory valuation is not on a LIFO basis, is there any reason why is should not be put on LIFO? Also, of particular importance in this era of inflation will be an analysis of the difference between the depreciation being charged on an historical cost basis and the depreciation allowance that would be necessary to reflect replacement costs of fixed assets.

After making whatever adjustments in reported earnings are called for to take account of such factors, we would look at the revised profit margin before taxes. It is difficult to generalize, but if the company is about an average postwar performer in a reasonably prosperous industry, this pre-tax profit margin will very likely average between 10 and 20 per cent. For a selected group of leading manufacturing companies, the average margin after taxes has stayed close to 7.5 per cent in the postwar years, which is almost identical with the average margin in the best prewar years, the great difference in corporate tax load notwithstanding.

MEASURING RETURN ON INVESTMENT

Comparison of the profit margin of the company under examination with the margins realized by competitors will shed light on management performance and competitive position. However, the margin on sales is merely one of the two elements that together determine earning power. The other is the ratio of sales volume to capital investment. Where large sales volume is developed with a relatively small capital investment, even a low margin on sales may yield a very satisfactory return on the investment, and return on investment is surely the ultimate criterion of profitability.

⁋ THE AUTHOR

Robert F. Bryan has been a partner in J. H. Whitney and Company since 1948. He received his A.B. from Oberlin and his Ph.D. in Economics from Yale. After serving as instructor in economics at Yale and Princeton, he joined Lionel D. Edie and Company for one year before serving in the OPA. After a period as Chief Statistician with Goodyear Aircraft Corporation, he returned to Lionel D. Edie and Company as Assistant Vice President and then Vice President, before joining J. H. Whitney and Company.

There are several different ways of measuring return on investment, the most common of which is the ratio of net profits to book net worth —that is, the percentage return on the equity dollars that have been put at the disposal of the company to date. In using this criterion of earning power to compare different companies, one must keep in mind that two companies may have the same current sales volume, operating costs, and expenses and yet show quite different rates of return on net worth, simply because one built its plant at a lower price level than the other. This gives it the added advantage of larger earnings (because of lower depreciation charges and smaller capital investment). Returns on net worth are also affected by differences in capital structure, by differences in inventory accounting methods, and, at present, by differences in the excess profits tax base.

In the three highly profitable years 1947, 1948, and 1950, the average rate of return before taxes on book net worth for all manufacturing companies was 25.5, 25.6, and 25.1 per cent, respectively. The return on net worth after taxes in these three years was 15.6, 16.1, and 15.4 per cent. For a selected group of some 1,700 leading manufacturing companies the return on net worth after taxes in these same years was 17.1, 18.2, and 17.1, respectively. These postwar rates of return are overstated because book values of fixed assets are still in large part at pre-inflation costs, and depreciation allowances are on the same basis. In the best prewar years approximately this same group of leading manufacturing companies showed earnings of about 12 per cent on net worth.

The potential return to be realized by the prospective purchaser of a stock interest in an established company will, of course, be measured by the relationship of future earnings after taxes to the price he pays for his stock, rather than to the book value of net worth. The inverse of this return is the "price-earnings ratio" so commonly used in discussions of common-stock values. The price one will pay for past or current earnings of any company will depend primarily upon the prospects of future growth in earnings, the probable resistance of earnings to a cyclical downturn in general business, the rate of dividend being paid, the general financial condition of the company, and the returns available on alternative investments. Perhaps the most commonly used "median" yardstick for industrial common stocks over the years has been about ten times average earnings, while the range for different industries and different periods of stock-market enthusiasm has been from five to 20 times earnings. However, investors are always looking for stocks they can buy on the basis of, say, four or five times what they think future earnings are likely to be.

REVIEW OF CURRENT AND FIXED ASSETS

Earnings cannot be appraised without a careful weighing of financial condition as revealed by the balance sheet. The number one question here is whether short- or long-term debt seems excessive in relation to earning power. The usual checks are: Is working capital adequate; is the current ratio two to one or better? Has the recent turnover of inventory been satisfactory; has adequate provision been made for impending short-

ages of key materials, and are inventories well balanced? Are the receivables of good quality, and is the average collection period normal?

Naturally, creditors like to see a fat cash balance well in excess of apparent requirements, but a great surplus of cash sometimes raises questions. Is the management diligently seeking and planning ways of reinvesting that cash? Is there danger of a penalty tax under Section 102 for unjustified accumulation of surplus? Is the failure to pay a dividend commensurate with earnings having a depressing effect upon the market price of the common stock?

With respect to the plant and equipment of the company under consideration, a check must be made on capacity, physical condition, obsolescence, efficiency in relation to competitors' plants, and probable timing of needed replacements of major elements. As I have already indicated, the extent to which the accumulated depreciation reserves and current depreciation charges fall short of reproduction costs will be a major concern.

The results of such a review of current and fixed assets together with estimates of future sales will reveal whether or not the company in question is likely to need additional capital and, if so, how much and how soon. If new capital will be needed at an early date, the stockholders must be prepared either to place debt or preferred stock ahead of their common, to put in more common-stock money themselves, or to dilute their equity by sale of new stock to others.

CONCLUSION

When we complete this analysis we may not be certain as to whether or not we want to buy a piece of the company; but if these are some of the right questions, then the answers will help us to compare this investment prospect with other alternatives.

II. THE SECURITIES ANALYST

By Harold B. Dorsey

MY COLLEAGUE, Mr. Bryan, has ably presented the factors that must be considered by an investment analyst whenever he is appraising the value of the securities of a given company. My problem today would be comparatively simple if I could tell you that 25 years of investment-research work has enabled me to build up a table of standard ratios which would prove that each company's current assets should be some specified multiple of current liabilities; that its capital structure should have a specified ratio of bonds, preferred stock, and common stock; or that a good corporation management should be able to earn some specific percentage profit on the capital invested.

However, the practical experience that I have had in this work encourages me to emphasize the fact that reliance on standard measurements for comparison purposes often can be a dangerous procedure. I have

ound, in actual practice, that there are so many valid variations from the
tandard that the standard itself is rendered of little value.

A company operating in one industry can safely roll along with
urrent assets only a little larger than current liabilities, but that same
atio for a company operating in another industry would be catastrophic.
ome companies can safely have a fairly large percentage of their capital
tructures in senior obligations, but the same ratios would be very bad
or others.

Therefore, I do not feel in the slightest apologetic about the fact
hat I cannot present a standard set of measurements that could be adapted
o a practical utilization of the principles that were outlined by Mr. Bryan.
'o the contrary, I should like to emphasize my conviction that the manage-
ent's refusal to abandon its reliance on some of the static standards of
easurements should constitute a negative factor in the analyst's appraisal
f the value of a given company's securities.

HE BUSINESS CYCLE

The blunt fact of the matter is that we do not operate in a static
conomy, and therefore the use of static tools is simply illogical. I am
onvinced that the successful investment analyst must make full use of
he principles and approaches that have been outlined by Mr. Bryan—
ut with a common sense interpretation of the figures. However, I would
ke to present for your consideration today another element which my
rganization considers to be of primary importance at this particular junc-
ure—an element that concerns a static type of thinking.

In our conferences with corporation executives, we are now looking
arefully for some sign that management is giving full consideration to
he current status of the business cycle. There are those who would try
o convince us that once again we are in a new era—that the cyclical rise
nd fall of business activity, employment, commodity prices, and earnings
 a phenomenon of a decadent economic and social philosophy. In my
pinion, we are going to have business cycles of noticeable amplitude just
 long as human beings are conducting the affairs of the world.

UTLOOK FOR BUSINESS ACTIVITY

In our interview work with corporation managements, there seems to
e a rather broad feeling that a continuation of the upward trend in general
usiness activity is insured by the promise of rising defense expenditures;
nd, as a rather natural corollary, that there should be a continuation of the
sing trend in personal purchasing power. I believe that this perspective

THE AUTHOR

arold B. Dorsey founded the Argus
esearch Corporation in 1934. As Presi-
ent he directs the broad economic and
vestment research of the staff special-
ts and writes a weekly interpretation
f the economic forces bearing on investment policies. Mr. Dorsey is a graduate of New York University. He worked
for eight years for the Socony-Vacuum
Company and held various investment-
research positions with brokerage and
insurance firms before he launched the
Argus Corporation.

of business prospects is the basis for the plans of numerous corporation managements.

It is not my purpose to elaborate on the outlook for business conditions, but I can scarcely illustrate the point that I believe to be of major importance without touching on the subject very briefly. I would urge every business executive to make a study of the third-quarter figures for Gross National Product—the dollar measurement of the nation's total output of all goods and services—and then to use his judgment in projecting the level that each major component of Gross National Product is likely to reach by the middle of next year. I think all would agree that there will be a reduction in consumer expenditures for durable goods and in residential construction activity and that the contribution that has been made to business activity by inventory building would be lost to the total of GNP. A more careful analysis of the recent levels of expenditures for new plant and equipment, and the trend of these expenditures in the early part of World War II, would probably be convincing argument that such business expenditures are not likely to contribute as much to the total of GNP as they have recently. On the other hand, it would be necessary to add a figure to represent increased expenditures for the defense program. After balancing the minus factors against the plus factors, I should be very surprised if the Gross National Product figure for the middle of next year is any larger than the one shown for the third quarter of 1951.

In my opinion, Gross National Product in about the middle of next year could easily be lower than in the third quarter of 1951. The minus factors would represent the loss of profitable business, whereas the plus factor (government expenditures) would represent a low profit-margin addition.

Whether or not it is agreed that the general trend of over-all business activity is going to flatten or perhaps decline, I think it will have to be granted that it is at least a possibility. But that admission would seem to carry with it a recognition of management's responsibility to conduct a corporation's affairs so that it will not be hurt if an important setback should develop.

THE NORMAL COMPETITIVE CONDITION

It has been a long time since we have heard discussions about breakeven points. I have a feeling that many managements have not calculated the effect on profits of, let us say, a 25 per cent decline in volume, or what their companies' financial problems might be under those circumstances. I know for a fact that some managements are justifying their expansion of productive facilities by utilizing profit margins that could only be achieved when volume and profit margins are abnormally high. In these cases, no consideration seems to be given to the effect on competitive conditions of the increased supply of that particular product that they will develop by their own expansion.

A judicious decision to invest the stockholder's money in new plant facilities naturally should be based upon the rate of return that might be achieved with normal volume and normal competitive operating conditions. But, one of the very important components of this formula involves a consideration of the question: "What is the normal competitive condition?"

Each of us has his own idea about "normal." It is my view that it would be treacherous to consider the broad conditions of the last five years as normal, because it is statistically provable that the business activity recorded throughout that period could not possibly have been achieved without an unprecedented expansion of private debt. Regardless of personal judgments as to whether or not a noticeable business setback is impending, I think we all have to recognize that we have a practically uninterrupted five-year period of extremely high business activity behind us. The very duration of this period of prosperity by no means constitutes assurance that we have entered a period of endless prosperity.

SMOOTHING OUT THE CYCLE

Perhaps I should be apologetic for bringing up doubts about the prospect for steadily rising business activity. I do not enjoy business setbacks any more than anybody else. However, I do have a deep-seated desire to lend every aid in smoothing out the extreme peaks and valleys of the business cycles. It is my conviction that the only way we can make distinct progress toward that goal is to stop the excesses—the over-expansion of capacity and the over-building of inventories—when they first appear. After all, it is much more difficult to alleviate the tribulations of a business setback after it once gets under way; the effective time to attack the problem is when the maladjustment is being created. It is statistically provable that business expenditures for new plant and equipment are largest at the top of a cycle, when the costs of such expenditures are greatest; and capital expenditures are at their lowest point at the bottom of the business cycle when a given company can obtain more plant for its money. It would be a great help in smoothing out the fluctuations in the cycle if business would spend more at the low points. But this is not possible if the expenditure has already been made at the preceding high point.

DON'T BE CAUGHT OFF BASE

Because it has all the foregoing facts in mind, my organization is somewhat concerned about the nonchalant attitude adopted by some financial officers on the subject of the deterioration of liquid assets in relation to current liabilities and in relation to capital commitments. I am thinking at the moment of a fast-growing company whose midyear balance sheet showed current liabilities very substantially in excess of cash and government holdings. It is true that this particular company subsequently floated a large loan and worked its way out of a position that might have proven awkward. But, what bothers me is the fact that the Treasurer of this particular company told one of my colleagues that he believed that too much cash in a company's treasury was an unnecessary luxury. I believe that this kind of thinking is due to the fact that it has been so long since the company has had to cope with adverse economic trends that this particular executive has forgotten the fact that economic conditions can change and bring into play forces over which the management has no control. An investment analyst would certainly take into

consideration the distinct possibility that this particular company will be caught off base in the event of a major downward trend in business activity.

SUMMARY

I hope that my reference to the importance of recognizing the position of the economy within the business cycle will encourage some serious thinking about the responsibilities of management in coping with the many problems that may have to be faced if we encounter a deflationary trend in business affairs. Even if an adverse trend does not develop in the reasonably near future, we, as investment analysts, deem it to be a primary function of management to be constantly alert to such a possibility and its effect on the company's operations—especially on its financial condition and cash flow in relation to capital commitments for expansion and inventory policies.

III. THE ACCOUNTANT
By Alvin R. Jennings

DEPENDABLE financial facts are required to judge the effectiveness of management and are indispensable in appraisals of the soundness of business enterprise. These facts are recorded and expressed in terms of dollars. The usefulness of such data rests on an implied assumption that fluctuations in the purchasing power of the dollar will be so limited that they will have no important bearing on the utility of the facts for most purposes for which they are needed. When pronounced changes do occur, it is clear that caution must be exercised in interpreting accounting data.

Generally, the people who develop and use financial information are aware of that need. Too often, however, their concern seems to be concentrated on the problem of accurately interpreting the operations of the current period, and insufficient thought is given to corresponding facts and data of past periods. Doubtless this is because no one has yet devised a fixed standard which will permit expression of financial facts on a consistent basis.

Nevertheless, trends of earnings—and, to a lesser degree, of financial position—are often of greater import than the happenings of any one year.

⁋ THE AUTHOR

Alvin R. Jennings, a partner in the accounting firm of Lybrand, Ross Bros. & Montgomery, has been with that firm since 1926. He is now serving on the Council of the American Institute of Accountants. He is also chairman of the Committee on Relations with the Securities and Exchange Commission and its Subcommittee on Cost Principles, a member of the Committee on Professional Ethics, and immediate past chairman of the Auditing Procedure Committee. He is also co-author of the most recent edition of Montgomery's Auditing and has written numerous technical articles.

COMPUTING INVENTORY IN TERMS OF CURRENT DOLLARS

The two areas of the earnings statement and the balance sheet most affected by acute changes in the purchasing power of the dollar are those influenced by investment in inventories and fixed assets. The LIFO method of computing cost of inventories used in producing goods sold, tends to place that computation more nearly in terms of current dollars to a major degree, and hence to make it more consistent with revenues, than do other traditional methods. Nevertheless, LIFO as currently applied is not a cure-all. Like some miracle drugs, it has toxic effects which on occasion have been known to raise the old question of whether the cure was not worse than the complaint.

The opportunity for tax savings, rather than the urge to make financial information more meaningful, unfortunately appears to have influenced its adoption, to a great degree, by industry. Existing studies indicate that perhaps 30 per cent of the inventories of companies studied are based upon LIFO. This percentage has not changed greatly since 1941 and 1942, when the incidence of the adoption of the method was at its peak.

DEPRECIATING FIXED ASSETS IN A PERIOD OF INFLATION

The problem of dealing with the effect of any acutely fluctuating price level on policies of depreciation of fixed assets is more complex than in the case of inventories; and, accordingly, it is farther from a satisfactory solution.

In 1948, the American Institute of Accountants sampled opinions of business executives, bankers, economists, labor representatives, teachers of accounting, lawyers, security analysts, and government officials on this question: "Do you think that a substantial change in accounting methods is necessary to provide satisfactory reporting of current income, in view of recent changes in the price level?" There were six other collateral questions. Seven of each ten who responded answered in the negative.

Following its survey, in the fall of 1948, the American Institute Committee on Accounting Procedures expressed its opinion that no basic change in the accounting treatment of plant and equipment is practicable or desirable under then present conditions, to meet the problem created by the decline in the purchasing power of the dollar. The Committee recognized that should inflation proceed so far that original dollar costs lose practical significance, it might become necessary to restate all assets in terms of depreciated currency. This has been done in a number of countries.

In its release, the Committee recognized that the prevailing forms of financial statements may permit misunderstandings as to the amount which a corporation has available for distribution in the form of dividends, higher wages, or lower prices; and urged that stockholders, employees, and the general public be informed that business must be able to retain out of profits amounts sufficient to replace productive facilities at current prices, if it is to continue to function. Full support of the Committee was therefore given to supplementary statements, explanations, or foot-

notes by means of which management may explain the need for retention of earnings.

EFFECT OF FLUCTUATIONS ON INCOME

In the spring of 1947, the American Institute initiated a broader survey—an historical study of the subject of business income. The project was conducted by a study group comprised of representatives from many fields, including law, economics, and statistics. Other members were drawn from banking institutions and labor organizations, and representative business analysts and government agents were included.

The major part of the considerations of the Committee over the past four years have related to the effect of fluctuations of the dollar on business income. It is contemplated that the Committee's report will be issued in the near future. One of the conclusions reached by the Committee is that for the present it may well be that the primary statements of income should continue to be made on bases now commonly accepted, and that corporations whose ownership is widely distributed should be encouraged to furnish information that will facilitate the determination of income measured in units of approximately equal purchasing power and to provide such information, wherever it is practicable to do so, as a part of the material upon which the independent accountant expresses his opinion.

The American Accounting Association is an organization comprised largely of people in the field of teaching. Its Committee on Concepts and Standards Underlying Corporate Financial Statements recently issued a report on price-level changes and financial statements. In that report the Committee expresses conclusions which are substantially in harmony with those reached by the two American Institute groups to which I have referred.

INTERPRETATION OF FINANCIAL DATA

From the record it should be apparent that the accounting fraternity has been conscious of the need for protecting the utility of financial statements against the destructive forces of extreme fluctuations in the purchasing power of the dollar. No fully satisfactory solution has as yet been advanced, but methods of improving the interpretation of financial data which are developed by traditional methods have been sharpened. These problems are still important, and must continue to receive the most careful consideration of those interested in the development and use of financial statements.

In the meantime, a word of caution expressed by the president of one large company in response to the survey to which I referred earlier may, I think, be in order. His comment was as follows:

> Unquestionably changes in the price level during the past ten years have been a matter of concern to management. It seems to us that these changes have occasioned the need for a careful reappraisal of many business policies. We have concluded that the price fluctuations, as an economic development, are related more to prudent business administration than to accounting. Until we can devise some more stable unit of measurement than the dollar of changing value, the problem of interpretation will remain. In my judgment, tinkering with the generally accepted accounting methods of computing income is subject to possible abuse and must inevitably weaken public confidence in corporate reports.

IV. THE BANKER

By Roger F. Murray

UNDER CURRENT CONDITIONS, the commercial bank lending officer is likely to be even more inquisitive and searching than he usually is. We all know how much easier it is to move inventories, collect receivables, and keep a plant operating close to capacity under the boom conditions which have existed and which do exist in many lines of business today. The current record, or the record of the last five years or so, may not be too informative on the question of how the operation is likely to look when and if the present period gives way to one of considerably lower activity.

The commercial banker, of course, has varying degrees of concern as to what the future may have in store. An adequately capitalized commodity dealer who knows the business and operates on a conservative basis is, after all, not too vulnerable to the kind of major change in business conditions which occurs from time to time. In most cases, his transactions will have been carried to completion in a matter of a few months.

FACTORS AFFECTING CREDIT

The problem of appraising a loan application becomes increasingly difficult as the period of financing is lengthened, and as the production or service financed becomes more highly specialized. In a manufacturing operation, for example, the lending bank wants to be quite well informed on four principal factors affecting credit.

First, knowledge of and confidence in the group managing the enterprise are absolutely essential. This is not simply a matter of being satisfied as to the integrity of one or two of the principals. Obviously, confidence in the fair dealing of the company is fundamental. But the banker wants to feel that there is a competent group of executives and a supporting staff which has the breadth of experience and the alertness to face the kinds of problems which are not even visualized at the time the undertaking is financed.

Second, quality of product, its acceptance in the trade, and its competitive standing are points on which the bank will wish to satisfy itself.

Third, the lending bank must be satisfied as to the soundness of the particular project which it is asked to finance. Obviously the banker is not an expert in every line of business conducted by his borrowing cus-

---

¶ THE AUTHOR

Roger F. Murray has been with the Bankers Trust Company since 1932, with time out for military service in the last war. From 1946 to 1949 he was Vice President in charge of the Credit and Investment Research Department. Since 1949 he has been Vice President in charge of the Economics and Business Research Department. Dr. Murray holds his B.A. from Yale and his M.B.A. and Ph.D. from New York University Graduate School of Business. He is the author of several articles for business and financial publications.

tomers, but he usually has within his organization considerable background material on the major industries, and he has a good deal of practice in appraising the soundness of a project. He is especially trained by every-day practice in the evaluation of financial officers as they present their plans.

Fourth, the bank lender wants to feel that his borrower does a sound and practical job of financial planning. It is most reassuring to the pros-pective lender to be presented with a carefully prepared financial pro-gram and estimate of requirements. The question of the cost and budget system in use is especially germane to the quality of the presentation. It may not be too important, from the standpoint of the soundness of the loan, whether a cash-flow projection happens to be moderately inaccu-rate. However, if it reflects a poor quality of financial planning and a poor organizational effort, it certainly tends to undermine the confidence of a bank-officer.

Everyone knows that a number of changes and revisions must be made in any financial plan because of unforeseen and unforeseeable con-tingencies. What disturbs confidence in the organization, however, are the changes and revisions which are made necessary by either inaccurate or incomplete preparation of the program in the first instance.

THE VOLUNTARY CREDIT RESTRAINT PROGRAM

At the present time, there is one additional factor to be considered in the granting of credit which does not ordinarily exist. That is the question of the purpose of the loan: Will it contribute to defense activity or expedite the production and distribution of goods? If so, it probably meets the test of the Voluntary Credit Restraint Program. On the other hand, if the project is not productive or would have inflationary con-sequences, the loan application should probably not be made.

This additional factor is temporary, in the sense that it was recently added to the usual considerations for establishing credit worthiness, but it may be with us for an extended period of time if the cold war continues.

SUMMARY

To sum up, good financial management in the eyes of a lending bank may be defined as the ability to instill confidence and to preserve it over an extended period of time. It is essential, of course, not only to have a good financial program but also to present it effectively. A company's accountants can be of great assistance in this presentation, even though at times good financial management may dictate some departures from the strict interpretation of the rules recommended by accountants and the S.E.C. The handling of reserves for raw-material price fluctuations, and the accelerated depreciation of abnormal or excessive fixed-assets costs, are cases in point. The so-called all-inclusive income account does not make good sense in many instances.

In any event, the effort of financial management should be concentrated on making its presentation as clear, consistent, and accurate as possible. All efforts in this direction will be amply repaid by the confidence engendered in the commercial loan officer.

DISCUSSION

DETERMINING CASH REQUIREMENTS

Question: Is there some objective test for determing the amount of cash a corporation should have?

Mr. Dorsey: I would say that the best way to determine how much cash you should have is to use common sense. You know what your monthly expenses are, you know what your sinking-fund requirements are, and you know how to anticipate your tax liability. Make certain that you have enough cash to cover these items and allow a fair margin over that amount for contingencies.

Dr. Murray: Perhaps that question can be answered by applying the liquidity test which is often used in the banking business. You total cash and receivables (presuming that you are satisfied with the quality and the collectability of the receivables), deduct them from the total of current debt, and then see how much your remaining current debt leans on inventory.

Obviously, there are varying rates of inventory turnover and different degrees of liquidity, but this method gives some rough measure as to whether you are leaning excessively on inventory to meet your current obligations.

Basically the reason you want to have the cash is to insure your ability to meet your current liabilities as they come along. This idea of the extent to which current liabilities lean on your least liquid assets—that is, your inventory—seems to me to be a good test for determining cash requirements.

Question: What is a fair relation of cash to current liabilities?

Mr. Bryan: I will discuss this in terms of a hypothetical, cross-sectional company that has perhaps 60 per cent of its total assets in current assets and a current ratio of 2¼ to 1. I would think that such a company, under present conditions, might have possibly half of those current assets in inventory, 20 or 25 per cent in receivables, and the balance in cash or U. S. government securities. That cash plus securities would be about 75 per cent of current liabilities, if my mathematics are correct.

I believe that for all manufacturing corporations in 1939 the ratio of cash and other liquid assets to current liabilities was about 50 per cent. During the postwar years, that ratio increased to about 100 per cent. It has been dropping, particularly during the last 12 to 18 months, and I think that for all manufacturing corporations it is now approximately 75 or 80 per cent.

If I regard that as typical, then, of course, anything that departs from

it will be subject to some examination. There is really no standard on a question of this sort. It depends entirely upon the showing of the company—its income statement and other conditions.

INVENTORY CONSIDERATIONS

Question: On the assumption that (1) finished products cannot be replaced at a lower cost, and (2) that the inventory content is of good, clean, saleable merchandise, what is the merit of having cash in lieu of inventory? Couldn't more sales opportunities be capitalized by selling from inventory rather than by planned production schedules?

Mr. Dorsey: It is true that a company can take care of some of its sales by liquidating its inventory and restoring its cash position. But, generally speaking, the ratio of inventory to sales is high, and that ratio would be even higher if sales decline (which is not an impossibility). It is that factor which bothers us, especially if a company has high current liabilities to meet. Suppose it runs into trouble and its sales decline. The ratio of inventory to sales looks bad, and the bank may suggest that some inventory be liquidated. The company than may be out of luck because its inventory cannot be converted into cash.

Question: Is it possible that under the Last-In-First-Out method of inventory accounting the profits of the company may be manipulated to a large extent by buying or selling inventory on the last day of the fiscal year?

Mr. Jennings: I would say that this is actually done in some cases. As a matter of fact, that is what I had in mind when I said that LIFO has certain toxic effects. I do not mean to condemn LIFO as a basis for squeezing out changes in the price level, but I believe we should recognize the fact that this is one of the possible effects of its use. Under present economic conditions the depletion of the LIFO "pool" or "reserve" results in an increased profit. I would suggest that instead of entering this profit in the income account, it be kept as a separate item on the balance sheet for the replacement of inventory.

Question: Dr. Murray, what will be the attitude of commercial bankers toward short-term financing of inventories for manufacturers of seasonal consumer soft goods in 1952?

Dr. Murray: I think that the attitude will be just about as usual. The real question that is going to be asked in 1952 is basically: "What is your inventory situation?" The banks generally are not anxious to finance speculation in inventory. They are perfectly willing—as they always have been—to finance a seasonal movement of inventory. That is one of their basic functions. But I think that in 1952 the loan officer is going to want to know that it is a regular seasonal inventory accumulation, that it is in line with your own careful appraisal of your sales prospects, and that, in general, analysis of sales prospects seems to make good sense by the regular standards of judgment. You may be sure that there is no disposition to restrict inventories to the point where they will curtail opportunities for the business to operate successfully and profitably.

Question: Do you think that the inflation forces are so strong that where the price trend in general is going to be upward a company should increase its inventories?

Mr. Bryan: This question depends on one's judgment of the strength of inflation forces. I believe that the money supply is the basis for changes in the price level—the money supply, together with the willingness of people to hold cash balances. From 1939 to 1946, the money supply—demand, deposits, and currency—more than tripled, increasing from $33 billion to $110 billion. The price level had gone up, as of the beginning of 1946, by only about 30 per cent.

Since then the price level has gone up another 75 per cent, reflecting the previous increase in the money supply. The money supply since 1946 has risen only from $110 billion to about $116 billion. The relationship of money supply to gross national product indicates that, at this present level of prices, we have now reached equality with the money-supply increase which took place during the last war. Therefore, I think that the inflationary forces, basically, are really quite weak at the present time.

DEPRECIATION BASED ON REPLACEMENT COSTS

Question: Mr. Jennings, do you believe that more corporations would use accelerated depreciation write-off to take care of higher replacement costs if income tax regulations permitted higher rates? What is to be said for starting a campaign to try to get the Treasury to recognize depreciation based on replacement?

Mr. Jennings: I think that more people would be interested in accelerated depreciation if the resulting larger amounts were permitted as deductions for tax purposes. Of course, the tax law already recognizes the principle; for example, it allows amortization in five years on facilities covered by certificates of necessity.

However, I think that we should exercise some caution in campaigning for changes in the law because if the Treasury recognizes depreciation based on replacement, they would then probably exact a capital gains tax on the unrealized appreciation of fixed assets. That has been true in several countries in Europe, and I understand that it has been included in the new tax structure in Japan. Corporations are being allowed to revise their assets in recognition of the depreciation in currency, but they are going to pay a capital gains tax on the increase in value of assets.

Question: Mr. Jennings, does the accounting profession have any objection to a company taking depreciation on replacement value, even if it is not tax deductible?

Mr. Jennings: That practice is not sanctioned at the present time by the general body of accounting principles. I think there has been a recognition of the fact that there is a method for accomplishing substantially the same result by accelerating depreciation in the early years by relating depreciation to economic life rather than to physical life, when there is a reasonable expectancy that the earnings in those early years will be at an abnormally high level. Such a policy is used by a number of companies, including, I understand, the steel industry.

REPLACEMENT OF EQUIPMENT

Question: Mr. Dorsey, would you approve of a major investment at this time to replace archaic production facilities with a new plant which on paper will pay for itself in one year? It may be necessary to borrow money for this project.

Mr. Dorsey: I do not see how anybody can criticize the replacement of inefficient equipment when it will pay for itself in that length of time, or even in two or three years. Nothing can be said against that as long as the market will take your commodity at a profit that will enable you to meet your new financial obligations.

Here again, I would say that it is just a matter of common sense. I think you should consider all the factors. You should remember that at the present moment your volume, generally speaking, is abnormally high; and since you have been operating in a seller's market, your profit margin may be high. If your production from that new piece of equipment is going to enlarge the supply side of the supply-and-demand equation for that commodity, do not forget to anticipate the possible effect on the price structure.

Question: Don't you feel that a machine replacement purchased today adds sufficiently to efficiency and capacity, as a result of technological improvements, to offset the so-called higher replacement cost?

Mr. Bryan: I think that may undoubtedly be true. It is true, for example, that since 1939 we have had an increase in the real output per capita of about 40 per cent as a result of technological improvements, and that compares with an increase in the general price level of about 90 to 100 per cent since that date.

MEASURING THE EFFECTS OF INFLATION

Question: So far as you know, are security analysts or bankers actually making comprehensive adjustments for price-level changes in the financial data which they may be using? Is it sufficient for their purposes to say that profits are materially overstated because of price-level increases, without making an attempt to measure this overstatement?

Dr. Murray: Any attempt to make any sort of a precise adjustment is extremely difficult because, supposedly, if you are going to adjust the past record and the statements in any way, you must have some notion of what you think is a normal price for the product.

I think it is more important to be generally aware of this price element in the picture, rather than to do a terrific amount of work, probably on the basis of rather sketchy assumptions, to try to adjust the data. You would not have very much confidence in the result after you were finished. Probably you could not get more than a few people at one time who would agree that you had done the adjustment properly, and you probably would not have gained much over just a general judgment.

Mr. Dorsey: The analyst studies the gross profit margin, and one of the peculiar phenomena of the last 18 months has been the very sharp widening in the profit margin. If the analyst does not watch his step, he will say that the widening was due to some factor such as a seller's market. However, I have always encouraged my analysts to recognize that the widening in the profit margin must have been due to some extent to a hidden inventory profit. This is another way of taking the rising price trend into your calculations. The controller at one of the large electrical-equipment companies told us that during the second quarter of 1951 most of the analysts who had talked to him had failed to consider the degree to which earnings were increased by a hidden inventory profit that would not ex, ⊦ in the second half of the year.

We do not make a precise calculation of the effects of inflation, but we do take into consideration the effect that the rising price structure and the decreased purchasing power have had on earnings and on every segment of the economy.

Mr. Bryan: The kind of adjustment that we make is similar to the one that Mr. Dorsey and Dr. Murray talked about—not any exact calculation, but a general consideration of inflationary effects. I think equally important as the inventory profits has been the high rate of return on net worth that is reflected in figures for the postwar years, resulting from the fact that the book value of fixed assets reflects, to a very large extent, pre-inflation costs. That greater return on net worth is something that is abnormal.

Question: Considering the effects of inflation, is there some fair basis for comparing current financial statements with past statements?

Mr. Bryan: It would seem to me that the first thing you would have to do, for a really perfect job, would be to state each year's figures in terms of contemporary dollars, so that for each year you have a statement of income in dollars of that year's value or purchasing power. Then you would have to compare each year's statement in contemporary dollars to some base dollar figure. When you get all through, I think you should have a complete picture of the effect of inflation.

SALE OF STOCK VS. BANK FINANCING

Question: A company wishing to increase its equity capital wants to issue preferred stock at the same time that it issues debentures. Is there some way of determining by ratio how much the issues should be in each case?

Mr. Bryan: I think the answer to that one cannot be specific. You must think in terms of what the over-all earnings coverage is of the interest requirements on the debentures and the dividends on the preferred stock.

At the present time, good coverage performance for an industrial company is something like an over-all coverage of 10 or 12 times. That would be for a preferred stock that yields about 4 per cent.

How you decide on the relative proportions, I do not know. I would say that, despite the allure today of the excess profits tax advantage in using debt, I would be inclined to stick to conservative principles and make the debenture issue as small as possible.

Question: A chemical company in the 82 per cent tax bracket needs substantial new money for expansion in 1952. Present capitalization is 40 per cent long-term debt, 10 per cent preferred stock, 50 per cent common stock, and surplus. How much more debt can be incurred currently in the form of convertible debentures?

Mr. Dorsey: I can see the big tax appeal in raising new money through debentures. I think there are some phases of the chemical industry that are cyclical, and that has to be taken into consideration. This idea of taking advantage of the tax factor by borrowing more money can be carried too far. However, I would not quarrel with 50 per cent in common

stock and 50 per cent in combined debt and preferred stock for a stable industry.

Conservative judgment would say that the company should sell more stock. If I were treasurer of the company I would try to calculate how bad my earnings could get. Then I would see how my charges might be covered. If I still arrived at a satisfactory answer, then I would feel that perhaps the company could safely increase its indebtedness.

Chairman Bogen: There is a tendency at times to put too much emphasis on the fact that the payment of interest is a deduction from taxable income. With an 82 per cent tax rate the Treasury is kind enough to pay most of the interest, in effect. But, we must always remember that the repayment of principal is not deductible from taxable income, and must ordinarily come out of earnings after taxes.

Question: At what point in a company's growth should it increase its capitalization through the sale of stock issues instead of bank financing?

Mr. Bryan: I would say that at the beginning of its growth it should certainly obtain capital through the issuance of stock. Later, it is a matter of deciding what kind of an equity capital base is justified by the size of the business. If, having attempted to avoid dilution by financing through the banks, you have reached a point at which the size really requires a larger equity capital base, then you must raise more capital. One other consideration is that the condition of the stock market at certain times may make it possible to raise equity capital on very attractive terms.

Dr. Murray: I believe that the answer hinges on one word—flexibility. In other words, at some point in your financing program, if you do not provide equity, you may very well (by reason of the accumulation of long-term and short-term debt) interfere seriously with your ability to take advantage of the new opportunities and to undertake new projects. It seems to me that you must always have the ability to borrow. There should always be some margin that you can call upon if a project turns up that looks promising. If you are using your debt-creating power or your credit standing to the limit, obviously you are severely restricting that flexibility.

SOUND MANAGEMENT ENCOURAGES INVESTMENT

Question: Mr. Bryan, do you consider a review of management policies pertinent to your conclusions about the desirability of investing in a company? What weight do you give to a company's labor relations? Are the long-range potentialities of a research program considered?

Mr. Bryan: We attach tremendous importance to sound management, even to the point of studying management first, and then determining what kind of a company the management has under it. Also, the record of labor relations is a very important one for us to look at.

In addition, we place a great deal of emphasis on research programs. No one can look at the experience of some of the chemical companies and ethical drug companies during the last few years without realizing how important to the investor that kind of research program can be, and how it can pay off many times over in earnings results.

PROVISIONS FOR RENEGOTIATION

Question: With a new renegotiation law for which regulations have not yet been issued, how are banks and security analysts appraising the possible effects of renegotiation on a company's liabilities?

Dr. Murray: That is really a troublesome question. We run into it all the time in trying to work out loan agreements, for example, in which there is some requirement for working capital. The question is: Should the best appraisal a company can possibly make of the renegotiation liability be added to its current liabilities? That would be a difficult question even if the regulations were all available.

Certainly the banks are very much interested in that question. Obviously, what appear to be free assets suddenly may be offset by liabilities after renegotiation.

Many companies, in a tentative or preliminary way, have been getting some indications of what profit allowances may be, and establishing some kind of reserve to cover possible liability. We do not care too much whether this reserve is shown on the financial statements; we can understand reasons, certainly, why companies may not care to incorporate even their best judgment on this subject in their statements.

Mr. Jennings: I think you are in a much better position to gauge the contingency now than you were in the early years of World War II. You do have a background for renegotiation, and, in my opinion, the approach to the problem administratively will be about the same as it was last time. If you are in an industry that was subject to renegotiation in the last war, you have a fairly good idea of what a reasonable percentage allowance may be.

On the question of the relationship of the problems to the financial statement, I would disagree with Dr. Murray in one respect. I think the statement should reflect possible contingencies. Of course, the area of risk is certainly considerably reduced now that the excess profits rates are so high, because obviously if you are going to give it back in renegotiation you are not going to pay as much tax.

I think the way to avoid this embarrassment that Dr. Murray refers to, is to make a combined provision for taxes and renegotiation, so that there is no separation between the two elements.

EFFECT OF INCREASED SAVINGS

Question: Mr. Dorsey, it is my understanding that the rate of personal savings has increased sharply during the second and third quarters of 1951. Would this additional savings have an effect in halting a business recession?

Mr. Dorsey: That subject of savings happens to be one of my pet peeves. I cannot think of any series of figures about which there is more misunderstanding than the Department of Commerce concept of savings. What they call personal savings has no relation to liquid savings. Their figures include such items as expenses for equipment for offices and farms, down payments on houses, and repayment of debt.

In the two middle quarters of 1951, liquid savings did rise—when the buyers went on strike. In other words, instead of putting money in merchandise, the consumer put it in the bank. Our studies show on a quarter-to-quarter basis, therefore, that it is quite likely that some of those savings came out in good Christmas business. When a study is made on an annual basis, the liquid savings are not running so very high.

If you consider the total liquid savings in the hands of individuals, and think of that in terms of the purchasing power for buying common stock (which so many people have in mind), the savings would not seem very high because prices of stocks have gone up. In other words, people are overlooking the economic function of price, which is a great leveler of supply and demand. I think that the figures are out of all proportion. You cannot look at the supply of dollars alone—you have to look at prices, too.

There has been a little increase in liquid savings that should keep us from the sort of depression that we had in 1932, but I do not think that the increase would be sufficient to prevent a business recession such as we had in 1937 and 1938.

Chairman Bogen: I have tried to find this increase in savings of about 250 per cent that the Department of Commerce reported for the latest quarter over a year ago. I cannot find them in the statistics of money in circulation; I cannot find the added savings in the reported deposits of the banks; I cannot find them in the insurance companies; and they are certainly not being used to buy savings bonds. They can only be found in the statistics.